DIARY

Marisa Crawford

SPUYTEN DUYVIL

NEW YORK CITY

CONTENTS

Remember Me   1

SPRING IS HERE AGAIN

Spring Is Here Again   9

I'm Too Sensitive for This World / This Foot Locker   11

Holy Sonnet   12

Choose Yr Own Adventure   14

I Was Gonna Buy a Blender Buying
    the Blender Would Be Self Care   16

Fuck You Allison   17

Freddy Krueger Is a Cutter   18

Zack Morris Cell Phone   20

BIG BROWN BAG

[I got the long, black dress]   27

[Kelly you don't realize I'm writing this]   28

[Everyone at Bloomingdale's]

[Otherworldly whimsy]   31

[Sometimes when I'm at work]   32

[My Bloomie's bag was]   33

[Oops I tripped and fell]   34

[Don't let me cry at the party]   35

[I thought of something]   37

[I bought the earrings]   38

[At the bus stop we were all]   39

[Working from home]   41

[My pilly cardigan]   42

[I remember when I used to work there]   43

[I was looking at the woman]   44

[I hate going into stores]   45

[I made the whole creative team die]   46

[Don't go in J Crew]   47

[Some songs are called "The End."]   48

[I got an email with the subject line]   49

DIARY

Diary   53

That I Would Be Good   56

45 Billion Observations While

    Listening to Indigo Girls Spotify Station   58

Diary   61

You Turn Me On I'm a Yellow Sony Walkman   64

Diary   65

Poem After One Jack & Ginger While

    Home Alone Listening to Steve Miller Spotify Station   68

Diary   72

Notes   76

Acknowledgements   78

Remember Me

Diary   /   Dracula Drive

I don't wanna go back to Connecticut I wanna go back in time

You've been watching me do my dumb dance moves for 20 years

We high five as you pass by

All the lip glosses come in new flavors for a new millennia

Putting on lipstick in the lobby or

Is it the opposite

This one's called remember me

It goes a little something like this

Holy smokes, I'm not a ghost

You can see me when I'm walking

around in your apartment

I ask my mom about God

She quotes the show *Friends*

I'm lying on the floor & I'm a body

I'd drunk dial someone but I don't know who

I'd find myself under the Christmas tree

Dedicate my whole practice to my father's brother

Text his ex-wife a Bitmoji

me with confetti

I say, the ghost is dissolving in the water

& it's a sad song

I want you to

remember me

*

How gross could a human girl get

Toasting marshmallows over a BIC lighter

Lying in the backseat with my head in your lap

like your parents didn't know what that meant

Cool cooler

Trying really

Got lunch w my dad, left

feeling sad then got cat-called

so hard it threw me half a block

Got cat-called again

I guess that to be the spokesperson for your generation

You have to be kind of outspoken

Or maybe just too drunk or fucked-up to care

In the wind / I think I got blown over by you

& that is how I ended up here

A cigarette in one hand & a Christmas garland hanging on you

Lives trying to be too epic

Or just too fuct up to care

*

I think that my mom was terrified

Raising 3 girls alone

She was like Drew Barrymore in *Scream* all the time

I'm having a hard time existing

The sunset & stuff

Sometimes I send you random texts like

Just went for a run on the track

Just to try to cultivate a relationship like that

I google my ex-boyfriend

I google my other ex-boyfriend

I listen to music on my yellow Sony Walkman

"But I wasn't a bad girl. I don't want to be forgotten."

Got kissed on the movie theater steps by the flagpole

Had an epiphany with Marc's fingers in my mouth

Where's the AIM I'm lost

I'm six girls all at once

Sad store where we ate sad breakfast bagels

I once performed "Jenny from the Block" karaoke, it sucked

My mom is my ars poetica but not

Lost my sunglasses in the ocean

Remember me

Remember me

Remember me

SPRING IS HERE AGAIN

Spring Is Here Again

I wave to you from inside the 90s
You want me to be a phenom or you want
me to wait until I'm older
You wrote on my Facebook wall on
my birthday, "here's to aging gracefully"
I wanted to reply "fuuuuuuuck youuuuuuu"
Buy me gold jewelry
The Misfits lead singer should have been me
You call your commute to work
an "odyssey" / it's not an odyssey
It's a picture of your newborn baby
Boys I wanna hate in bloom

I think about the sea-green dress with
the poppy-red flowers on it, the one
that got away / how A told me it looked
"just okay." Maybe she was right. Maybe
I'll drift down with the undertow
I'll gasp for air. Chloe.
I'll never know.

Balcony scene
First-season Miranda
Gotta send the invoice gotta change my tampon
Maybe he hates me for not being nice enough
or maybe he doesn't hate me at all
My face flanked by Only Ours symbols

My nose won't stop bleeding
I haven't been partying. The Big Wind Blows
for whoever partied last night

I need a job so I'm not alone when the world
is ending. Hey guys I'm here I'll just sit over here

I can't work here anymore. I collapse in
a glass coffin. How do you make your
skin look youthful without being young
Expressing myself joyously through fashion
Wearing whatever the fuck I wore yesterday
When I started my job I made my password
96tears. Now it's 113tears

Everyone around me is smoking
Lean against the wall like you're one of the flowers
That's called "personification"
or maybe "objectification"
Embodying the statue
of the saddest girl on the block
Turning passers-by to stone
w/ my bald eye

I'm Too Sensitive for This World / This Foot Locker

Oh right, the bomb
Sorry so boring
300-year-old wiener dog
China teacups rimmed in gold
Oh right, underwater
Backwards somersault, no
Outside w/ the flowers
Uhhhhhhhhhhhhhhh like it matters
9th grade Metallica disaster
Cutest hottest-pink dress ever
Janie / not Janie / not over
Summer that bled into forever
See that backslash that's the gash in my left arm
See that scar that'll always be there
Janie would be like, so stop doing it
So eat something, J
So coconut cake bonne bell
You shoved it in my face / posted on my wall
Smell it, smells like a memory
Smells like a fake cake
This metal gate has been a gift to me
That metal guy at the party with the long hair and the gift for
Piercing the beer can / swallowing it all in one gulp
Was that the first time
He like, put his arms around me from behind
Somehow I willed it to happen w/ my mind
& then there was / a porch swing
Macbeth, my whole life, my death, everything

HOLY SONNET

When I moved my bed into the middle
of the room, proclaimed I had fallen ill w love sickness.
It didn't last. After a week, moved it back.

My best friend hates me
My mom throws two sticks of gum in my bag
You buy me a package of sixteen
glittery butterfly hairclips
You drive the car forward an inch
every time I try to get inside

Even your aesthetic is violent
Even your baby in my stomach
Even the way you play the crossword
puzzle game & you always win

I've been invisible all day
& I want someone to see me
I am nearing the end of how I feel physically
The stairway behind the pool
on the south end of the school

Berry stains on my Birkenstocks /
How time stopped

You were in my class
I was your teacher
vice versa /
You asked me "are you sleeping" &
I answered with my eyes closed, "no"

I'm in Saint Patrick's Basilica throwing
my Christmas corsage at the Virgin Mary
I put my lipstick on w no hands
I gave a shout out to myself

Choose Yr Own Adventure

What if I was a little girl
Born in a post 9/11 world
Cartoon drawing with star earrings on it
Really don't wanna hear it

Why do I even work here
Who even am I
Archangel Lucifer
Things that shoot across the sky

I started crying while I was brushing my teeth
when I realized I'm the same age D was when she died
Then I realized I'm actually one year older
which made me a) cry harder or b) jolt to a stop

The guy jackhammering the street outside
yelled "smallest hole ever," then hooted three times
Dad tells me I'm in my "working years"
I'm running for the train

The male comedian said we should all just walk around looking
for things to eat, then shit it out, it's that simple
Is it a) mansplaining life, or
b) secret garden overgrown w/ vines

I got this thing in a Cracker Jack box
I thought of my grandma's purple wallet
Plastic gem flowers blooming out of it
Balled-up dollar bills stuffed inside

I call back after the interview
Try soooo hard not to uptalk
A robin's egg blue tile
I found it in the dirt when I was five

I Was Gonna Buy a Blender Buying the Blender Would Be Self Care

I'm outside yr apartment leaning back against the Party City
with one knee up, smoking. JK not smoking.
I exhale smoke in a long bored line at you,
at all of you, at even the thought of you.

The only good thing in this whole wide world
is you throwing me birthday parties
Going out for coffee
Talking about Roe v Wade at Starbucks
Disappearing w/o a trace.
You kiss me outside the coffee shop,
the pastry shop, the candy shop.
It keeps getting sweeter & sweeter.

I'll sit on the stoop w/ my knees knocked together.
Light a candle for every time.
I catcalled a girl by accident.
She just looked so good.
It was like looking into an ivy wall.
Lush & green like you God.

You kissed me like a sidewinder.
You & what army of yous.
You told me I was a sad tomato.
Like me in my job interview dress but better.
Somehow barefoot in the middle of town in December
I bet I'm radiating light right now, I bet I am
A toy poodle in the sun
My shampoo bubbles
Drop a sugar cube into

Fuck You Allison

Allison would be like, what's grosser than gross?
Two eels doin' it in a bucket of goo.
& I don't even understand.
I don't even understand my own tattoos.
I wish that I could stop you from talking
when I hear the silly things that you say.
That was the only line from the song
that Dave said actually reminded him of Allison.
Be mean to the girls, they're band-aids,
they're pirates. Tiny dancers.
Like Amy was always so obsessed w/ how small I am,
once a cab driver in the Haight said, she's not *that* small.

We were walking around Brooklyn when Anthony
was visiting, saw graffiti of a hundred
"Fuck You Allison"s on a wall.
Shut up or it'll become a memory.

Allison would be like, wocka wocka wocka.
No Anthony *threw me* in the pool.
He followed me here.
He wrote on my Health quiz in 6th grade,
good job I'm really proud of you.
There was a wall in Allison's
bedroom, but it wasn't an emotional wall.
Last night I had a dream.
Got an astronaut tattoo.
Folded the note into a football.
Carried it around in my bra till now.

FREDDY KRUEGER IS A CUTTER

He loves to cut himself
In your dreams
Then laugh at how
He doesn't bleed.

I dropped my work ID in the middle of the street
It opened up a portal in the pavement
I know I said
that I was done
but I'm gonna keep goin'.

Things that grow out of pavement
Glittery tear that rolls out of my eye
Girls who dress for work like they're dressing
for the most important social event of their lives.

I'm disappointed with myself that I didn't
return the sweater, but happy with myself
for going to the gym.

I'm in the basement.
I'm in the clouds.
I'm in the bathroom
listening to all the pissing sounds.

Caught myself doing air guitar on the train to "Doll Parts" / couldn't stop.
Put my headphones on and somehow Ani was already playing / didn't
question it.
Cause there's a god.
Cause there is a goddess.
"Thank You" by Alanis.
They really want you but I do too.

"Doll Parts" makes me think of my
mom driving in the car in 1994.
Learning that every mom is not like your mom.
I went to college, I wrote a short story
called "The Pullout Method."
Learning how to wash your own clothes.

Woke up with an overwhelming
desire to wear the color purple.
Put on the paisley shirt Amick bought me at H&M.
Someday it'll be vintage.
Someday not that far away.
I remember when Tara turned 25 she posted "I'm officially vintage."
I remember when Jason used Amick's name in a poem.

Where have all the good men gone
& where are all the gods.
I wear these sneakers my sister bought me
that are so not me / but it's like I don't even care about my identity.
Wanted to listen to Bangles radio.
Love it in yr room at night.
In the dark I like to read his mind.
Story you'll tell your kid someday in a car.

I didn't get that Trivial Pursuit
was about it being trivial / still don't.
Felt like a game that was made for boys
in a world that's run by men /
Poem I wrote about Freddy
Poem I wrote about Jason
I listen to "Doll Parts" I think it is the 90s.
The pink one.
Cut me
another piece.

ZACK MORRIS CELL PHONE

It's not that I don't get it, it's that
I don't care. I see you calling &
I don't wanna pick up. You tell me
we won't be fifteen forever. Rows of girls drinking
ginger ale or water. Picture of me in princess
sleeves in 2005 / still alive.

If you could take the date stamp off the picture
put it in a time capsule.
The nail polish, I still have it.
Tori Amos with glitter.
The shade is called "caught a lite sneeze,"
No, "pieces of me you've never seen."

On the Tori Amos Facebook page
saw a post that said, pray for Joni.
I thought (you wrote a spell),
like witches believe in prayer.
Someone wrote, you should especially Tori,
you owe her your whole career.

With friends like these.
End of the world.
Gun that blows out bubbles
instead of bullets.
Timeless toy bringing
timeless groovy kinda joy.

I pulled out my phone & it
just looked like this, I
shocked myself / superfan.
Kelly Go Lightly.

Tear in my hand.

L said, I'm not your dog &
pony show. I said, yeah
you are. Now take me
to the faire.
I wanted to write you a poem
but I thought, so not
timeless. *Elle* editorial
on the season's best bralettes.

That woman, I said,
she's wonderful.
She's climbing the
corporate ladder.
She's wearing the blush neon
pink of the season.
She says there's a story
at every rung.

Oh hell, Helen. You didn't
have to go and do that.
Die with all yr
sisters watching.
Leave your voice recorded
in a box by the phone.

I wrote a poem about the breakup,
the baby as a metaphor.
How you were adopted
& how the last time we talked
you said you just wanted
to smash your phone.
Oh hell, time.

Oh, somewhere or another.
Our feminist friendship
has been such a pleasure.
At your mother's house.
A long black dial tone.
Bottle of cologne that M wore.
Eau de Zack Morris Cell Phone.

I stole it from you, or
you stole it from me.
I had the *Saved by*
the Bell soundtrack on CD.
Used to listen to "Friends Forever"
driving to take the train to the city.
Tickets were $17.50.
Museum of Radio & TV.
Museum of when D jumped onto
the tracks to get me a washer
that I wore as a ring.
When I was seventeen.
Museum of D getting
down on one knee.

& that's what sad is.
& never get over it.
& all over the Internet.
Babies named Alice,
or Bernie or Billie.
Pulled down my panties,
found an inkblot.
Put the girl
in the now.
If she's there /
Pull up the
antenna.

BIG BROWN BAG

"Piece by piece, I fed my wardrobe to the night wind, and flutteringly, like a loved one's ashes, the gray scraps were ferried off, to settle here, there, exactly where I would never know, in the dark heart of New York."

—Sylvia Plath, *The Bell Jar*

I got the long, black dress. The dress that leads to nowhere.

I saw the Bloomingdale's out of the corner of my eye

& with the way the light was hitting it, it looked like a mirage.

A woman on the subway is crying.

Jenny wants to live forever in the city. Just going &

going & going like a road that leads to nowhere.

Jenny used to say if you rub your hands together, then hold

them still, you can feel the vibrations of the earth's foundation.

That's what we did in California, with our bodies.

We rubbed everything together all the time.

I saw the Bloomingdale's. It was an informant &/or a step.

I'll go there & I'll be invisible. My body will levitate

with wonder. It won't have to exist at all.

Kelly you don't realize I'm writing this

cause if you did you'd be laughing out loud.

If my hair looks bad, it's cause I had to write

the poem. If the poem seems short it's cause

I had to write the copy. If I'm wearing

the wrong shoes it's cause I had to run

for miles. If there are no men in this poem

it's cause they all walked out.

Sometimes I feel invisible no matter how

big the bow on my headband is.

No matter how gold my platinum glows.

People think I'm wearing all black cause

I work at Bloomie's. Fog in front of full moon,

whatevs. I'm wearing all black in mourning.

Everyone at Bloomie's is pregnant

with evil Satan babies, or promo codes,

sharp-edged pairs of shoes.

I said hi to you through

the deep wade of my purple lace.

I picture myself sitting down on a

corner. Giving birth to a feeling.

Rainbow butterflies. I look in all the

windows, looking intentionally sad.

Like, my sadness is a choice.

O moody tearful night.

Blush pink tulips

faint across the dumb garden.

Smell of lilac fills the room.

My dad looks up at the sky,

compares it to the sky on 9/11.

It's never as bright, it's never as blue.

Me in the UMass library in 2001, looking down.

Me kissing a rose in a garden in Spain, 2002.

Otherworldly whimsy. Blushing toward a feeling of death.

Clothes that look severely expensive. Luxury brands that aren't really a luxury at all.

If you buy the perfume today, you essentially get a goody bag with it.

Buying clothes you don't like. Running up the stairs to a job you hate.

On the subway, one hunched over old man gave up his seat to another hunched over old man.

The woman who hates Bloomingdale's so much she broke the elevator with the power of her hatred.

I was wearing the Smashing Pumpkins ZERO shirt.

I was in ISS and the Unabomber was bombing and you were somewhere, looking for me everywhere.

I was wearing the argyle sweater we passed around in the 8th grade.

Janie's hair when she wore it. Dave's braces when he wore it. Jes's rings when she wore it. Even God wore it.

I was in the bathroom channeling Janie's mom's bathroom.

I was in the conference room channeling Ariel.

I was wearing jeans as blue as a housewife in the 50s.

I fell backward on the train like I was in a mosh pit, and the crowd saved me.

Sometimes when I'm at work I say things like please

superscript the R-ball and add dims to the dot whack, thanks.

Jenny put ketchup on her burger in the shape of a smiley face.

Everyone at Bloomingdale's is watching their weight. And I'm

no better. The way I spilled my coffee down my shirt.

How my boobs move when I walk. I found a dead cockroach

in the sink this morning. Its antenna didn't register me.

I'm a Gemini, I'm a goddess, I'm a medium.

Alligator shirt I bought you at the store under the train tracks.

Jay, I miss you. I miss the "idea" of you. I miss the feeling

of it slamming around in my head. I'm a loose

woman, you guys. I had an epiphany in the garden.

I look good in antiqued things. Gatherings.

Body like a golden pear, or ringing like a bell.

My Bloomie's bag was flapping in the wind like a weapon.

I didn't want to wait for traffic so I just walked right in.

Sometimes when I'm walking in the woods I think about Bloomie's.

And I get weak in the knees.

Sometimes when I'm in the hall taking a call I feel the whole building vibrating deep in my body like a guitar string.

They say that Bloomingdale's is like no other store in the world.

That New York City never sleeps.

Two truths and a lie.

My great-grandfather was the elevator man in the Flatiron Building.

My grandfather was the mayor's chauffeur.

My grandmother was a Rockette.

On our first date I felt like throwing up and you told me to stare at the yellow line.

In the city car my dad let me use the siren, pointed at the antennae in the sky.

All the things I didn't say.

All the things I didn't buy.

Oops I tripped and fell out the third story window of Urban Outfitters.

At the time I was wearing an "Urban Renewal" repurposed

flannel which was just a shirt that I actually owned in the 90s.

The music that came on sounded like angels singing. I landed

on the street across from the Bloomingdale's holiday display.

I held up the shirt to my body in the mirror. I felt

righteously disgusted & also disgusting.

It's my lunch hour. I stopped breathing.

The shirt was so soft I started crying.

The poster says war is over, but it isn't.

I have a gift card, my dad bought me it for Christmas.

Don't let me cry at the party.
Don't let me drink like a monster.
Make time stop. I was so bad
I made time stop.
Hyphen this, hyphen that.
I looked so all-American in the picture of us
where your finger was up my nose.
If you miss me, just say so. With your arms.
Ring a bell. I sang, I'm proud to be an American,
ironically. I cried a single space shuttle tear.
I killed the fruit fly with a Starbucks napkin while saying,
"bitches get stitches."

Rebecca on the phone at work said
the landing page was halted, I heard "haunted." I'm a creep.
How I think about you at night when the world's ending.
Oh it's one o' clock. Oh I'm thirty.
I live in New York City. My hair is turning gray
with excitement, Leland Palmer style.
In 8th grade words felt edgy. People had secrets.
Scary feelings filled the room like shadows.
Music from violins.

I'm talking to myself in front of the bike shop.
I'm channeling Shannon Hoon eating corn on the cob
in Janie's closet. I'm channeling myself
in 2007 getting ready for the party.
I'm projecting outside my body so far.
Separated-at-birth twin sisters connected by
long bungee cords on the astral plane.

You caught me repeating the name of the lost
dog on the poster. I reached into my bag
for my phone, and pulled out a Kit Kat.

The pile of mail has gotten too big to look at.
The FDNY shirt has too many holes to wear.
The astral plane has gotten too hard to navigate.
Too many places to see while I'm there.

The girl at the MAC counter made my makeup look
like Amy Winehouse's, so now I have her song
stuck in my head. And I keep singing it out loud in public,
which is stupid, cause my makeup looks like hers.
Oh we miss you Amy. We miss you childhood.
We miss you parties. Miss you Tiffany Blue.

I thought of something but now I forgot it.

How my boss and my sister went to college together.

How I met Katie in the year 2000 and since then we

have both moved forward in two straight but totally

separate lines that revolve around the sun in orbit.

I am sitting at my desk & I'm sitting in outer space.

I had this idea but then it floated into the ether.

The only way I could get to work was

to turn off my brain and be dumb, dumb, dumb.

And then my brain got stuck there.

I'm texting in the middle of the street I'm so dumb.

I'm slamming against the hoods of cars I'm such a dummy.

I used to start all my letters with "I'm sorry." I'd seal them

in pretty envelopes and draw giant S's on them.

Sorry, sorry, sorry, and bright and shining.

I'm standing in the street and all the cars

are coming. Oh well, I tried. At least

I tried. That's more than I can say about you.

I bought the earrings cause I was sooooooooooooooo bored that the boredom carried me into the earring store.

I'm sorry to the giant antique urn. I'm sorry to the magic.

That every single day I obscure by floating above the sidewalk in all black like a ghost on my way to buy the earrings.

Every time you were above me it was like there was a spirit hovering over me. Like there was a demon inside me.

I don't know where you are and the search for you possesses me. The search for you is rattling in me.

When I first met you I was like, oh, I found you. Thank god I found you. You're finally here, I am finally here.

I am floating toward the earrings and I am pulling toward the world.

The hot pink flowers like rich girls. Ripe fruit. Who sit outside all day with the flowers.

I was so scared. I pulled the car to the side of the road.

Where the Pequonnock used to live. Where the insane asylum used to be.

Where the white lady used to glow in the mist.

When we were on our way home from Newtown.

And I tried to smoke the bowl. I was scared there was nothing left.

At the bus stop we were all,

check it out I'm smoking! And then

we'd exhale visible breath into the icy air.

Later we were all, does smoking warm you up

I'm freezing. Then we started smoking.

In *The Breakfast Club* Ally Sheedy says,

when you grow up, your heart dies.

I won an award at work today,

I was all, oh my god

you guys you shouldn't have!

No really, you shouldn't have.

I had my hands in the sink,

a braid in my hair. I think

that I'm closer to God that way.

Janie thought that in *The Breakfast Club* Ally Sheedy

looked better before Molly Ringwald gave her a makeover,

but I thought she looked good both ways.

When you're crossing the street during

rush hour you might feel like you're invincible,

but you aren't.

Your heart doesn't die.

You haven't "worked late."

I hold my Bloomie's bag in front of me like it's a bomb.

I hold the emergency door open

for the teenagers sneaking onto the subway.

Cause I'm cool like that.

I drop a penny down the grate.

Working from home I take a "lunch break"

that involves me eating mac & cheese straight

from the pot. It makes a warm feeling

traveling down to my stomach.

In high school I'd try to go

the whole day without eating.

Then I tried being the cool girl

who doesn't care about getting fat.

I had a stack of *Seventeen* magazines.

A quart of Phish Food ice cream.

Smear of vanilla

lip gloss where my mouth should be.

My whole horrible life in front of me.

Row of manila folders.

My pilly cardigan. My pink birthday cake with fake roses. Somebody's "Heine."

We're all 30 / we're all dying / we all were born yesterday.

It's idiotic. How after you kissed me I stood around with my mouth hanging open for

days. My tits out like a nursing "mom" in the park. A nursing party girl.

I ran on the elliptical again & again & again but it didn't change anything.

He hit me with a bomb, I remember it.

Don't tell them to grow up, and out of it. Where's your gym at?

Where's the party, Sadie? Your hair had that hot honey halo in my dream

last night. I thought you were here when I woke up.

In New York City. I thought the light could carry me.

I remember when I used to work there. I don't work there anymore.

I could get hit by a car, it could kill me. All my bells & whistles & baubles.

The mallard dress that I didn't buy in 2005 was a major personal loss for me.

I willed the guy on the subway bench to move over with my mind.

Jay hates it when people move to new towns and make friends

with people they don't really like but I love it, I love it, I love it.

I went back a year later and the dress was on sale, so I considered stealing it.

I deserved it. I almost deserved it. For how that store treated me when I was in it.

Stacks and stacks of shoe boxes full of it. Left its weird seed in me.

How I took that job to make friends, and all the clothes lined up on the walls

converted me into something I never wanted to be. A blush piece of

fabric with eyelets along the bottom. A branch on a family tree.

I was looking at the woman in the subway station

playing "One Hand in My Pocket," and I slipped

on a French fry. Thought of the line, "I've got one hand

in my pocket, and the other one's eating a French fry."

I was hanging out in Duane Reade for an extra five

minutes cause the *Karate Kid* song was on. I have money,

I use it to buy mint chocolate chip ice cream-flavored gum.

I walk into the salad bar while the guy in front of me is

looking at the menu. He says, go ahead, and I say no,

go ahead, then he says, it's not that big a deal, and I say,

oh, fuck you. 40,000 women die of breast cancer each year

so my salad is in a bubble-gum pink container.

And I'm grossing myself out in my cubicle with

the sound of me chewing it. The man on the elevator says,

"you better put on your jacket it's cold out there."

Rebecca at work says she just doesn't see an end in sight.

To her workload. To the war. I saw you walking

toward me from across the street. I was holding my

Starbucks cup. Probably when I saw you, my eyes lit up.

44

I hate going into stores on my lunch break because

the thing that I want is something I can't buy in stores.

Maybe it's the hot rock gold ring that's shaped like

a skeleton key or maybe it's the black hair on your arms

when they're around me. Sometimes when I'm standing

in a ray of sun I google why does it feel so good to stand in the sun.

I imagine a time when I couldn't have anything I wanted instantly

and when things shaped like skulls reminded people of mortality.

The personality test I had to take to get the job I don't want

said to know yourself, know who are and be who you will be.

I know myself. Which is why I stand in a patch of sun like it's a spotlight

and stare in the windows of hair salons into my own eyes in the mirror.

Know who you are and what decade you're from and sit quietly

with the events that define that decade. Sometimes I see my family

members roaming around the city in formal clothes. I've watched

their hair and their bodies grow. My body grew too. I work in a

creative field, which means I get to wear more creative kinds of shoes.

I made the whole creative team die laughing

when I said, "I can't remember anything before

today." And then I looked at the bare white legs

under me, and at the gray ghost hovering

over me, and I got so embarrassed I got

"Going to California" stuck in my head.

I walked into the last stall on the right

like a zombie. I remember when Jay worked

at the bar, and I worked at the store,

and we joked about him mixing fake drinks,

and me filling a toy register with pretend money.

I think about that and I laugh so hard

that my eyes close, and tears pour

out of them. Crying over something

plastic and colorful. Something make believe.

Don't go in J Crew. It's too depressing.

Don't go into Bloomingdale's either.

Look for the hot guys. Look for yourself in the hot guys.

In the ice cream truck as it drives by.

We used to call the ice cream truck *Charlie*

cause that was the ice cream man's name.

And also what they called the enemy in Vietnam.

When I choked on the cupcake, I whispered,

I'm dying. When the plane hit the tower,

my dad knew without knowing.

When a bomb explodes, it makes a sound.

At Bloomie's all the women say,

keep me away from the cupcakes.

Keep the cupcakes away from me.

I was looking in all the windows.

The mannequin looked like you.

When you were sleeping, when you were leaving.

It looked like me too.

Some songs are called "The End."
They make everything seem so definite.

On Janet's last day the 9th floor smelled like popcorn.
All the Merch girls had eyelashes like mermaids.

Now that Janet's gone instead of chatting her
when I'm angry I do crazy things in Photoshop

like make a picture of the tabletop builder landing page
and write "TABLETOPOCALYPSE" across it in dripping blood.

Not that I think the apocalypse will be bloody, or that I will be there.
Not that I even know how to use Photoshop.
Not like anyone would even get the joke except for Janet, or maybe Jay.

The account manager said if the world was ending tomorrow,
we could go live with this project if we had to.
If aliens landed on the planet, said they were gonna blow it up.

Linda says her trainer says she doesn't eat enough,
and then she gets hungry and so she eats junk.

I made Janet a sign that said Interplanet Janet for her cubicle.
She was the only one that got it, and even she didn't really.

I made a name for the table with the swirling blue things on it.

Mom says the red M&Ms are poison / I used to believe her.

I hold my arms up like a radio antennae.
Whale sounds come out of the receiver.

I got an email with the subject line "10 signs your boss hates you"
If I were a boss I'd forward it to my direct reports.

Last night I remembered a bag of Reese's Peanut Butter Cups
in my cabinet, when I saw them I said "game changer" out loud.

When Jon Shina called Linens n Things "Linens n Shit,"
we were outside Van Meter, standing under a rainbow.

This was way before I worked at Bloomie's but after
9/11, before the secret Sonic Youth show at the Flywheel.

Just after Tara said, "mmm pizza" in her sleep but
just before the war, around the time when I smoked pot
and said, "aren't dogs weird?" on the bench outside Greenough.

At work, you can say "hey" sometimes.
You don't have to always say "hi" or "hello."

When you're fighting with your sisters or your roommates,
you have to just ride it out like a wave, or a pile of snow.

I used to work with a girl who said, "God forbid" about
everything. I got a company-wide email asking us
to back up our work just in case we're ever hit by a bus.

I don't use the word "beater" to talk about tank tops, and I try
not to say, "fight signs of aging" but sometimes I have to.

My coworker sneezed and I said "bless you," in the
voice of a guardian angel with wispy blonde hair.

There was that big sign on Route Nine that said, "Free Air."
Somebody told me, memory is a tire. Change it. Go from there.

DIARY

Diary

My nose is bleeding

Should I go see my *Sex and the City* doctor.

She'd be like, did you move here for a man or a job.

I'm walking in Midtown,

I'm like, good for you in your colorful outfit.

Sad for a sea of black.

I went to California with a youthful aching in my heart

and I left it there / didn't.

My sister's and my text relationship is so I do this, I do that.

I text her, I washed my new bra and it's so tight

I keep gasping for air in my cubicle.

She writes back, I fell asleep on the train

and when I woke up a spider was dangling in front of my eyes.

My cartoon world where I live with you.

Where I float across the ocean.

Where I miss my stop every day

but it doesn't matter / girl power.

Sometimes I post the things in my head

onto the Internet for a certain few.

For those to whom I'm like "good for you,"

your pastel dress in a sea of black

Maybe I'm like, hungry.

Gluten free Oreos. Can't hear myself think.

I'm listening to "Free Fallin'" on my Walkman.

I go into the grocery store and they're playing it too.

Cause I forgot the line & Tom Petty reminded me.

I wanna fly down over Mulholland /

wanna collapse on the grocery store floor.

The universe told me to go into the grocery store

and buy just cookies and milk.

D would've called it a "heroic purchase."

My therapist was like, maybe you're not over it.

The taste of the milk bored my tongue.

I'm walking around the grocery store.

"Epic" by Faith No More.

I'm running on the treadmill listening to

Lady Gaga and thinking about my sister.

And my sister calls and leaves a message

that she was listening to Lady Gaga

on the treadmill and thinking of me.

I text her two girls and two crystal ball emojis.

What if D dies.

And I'm like, how could you not need poetry?

Walking home w/ my grocery bag on my arm,

it feels like a tourniquet.

Use my computer as an extension cord.

Exercise or sleep.

You emptied the laundry all over the bed

and I screamed like a bomb exploded.

All the things that I'm interested in.

Will I take a selfie at the end of the world.

That I Would Be Good

I'm not trying to wear Nike sneakers around

the neighborhood but they're here

so I'm wearing them.

It's a cool look for a woman of my age.

I'll buy the mid-length black slinky skirt from Zara

& wear it around my apt in winter.

Problem w/o a name.

Forgot "Get into the Groove" existed

& now I'm sickened w/ myself.

Want an apartment with a backyard garden

& secret passage that leads into

an enchanted other dimension.

I hate myself I hate communication.

I'll put my phone in the kitchen cabinet like my mean

ex-boyfriend, go out all night kissing 21-year-old girls

w black bobs & burgeoning interests in Marxist

economics while I'm at home crying.

I'm a Gemini I'm splitting.

Twin girls / twin crystal ball emojis.

E was in the woods I was in my new apartment.

I was wearing Aimee's Betsey Johnson dress,

reading Betty Friedan.

That I would be good even if I got the thumbs down.

45 Billion Observations While Listening to Indigo Girls Spotify Station

Things that make me laugh: when Sarah McLachlan

says "there's no one left to finger."

How Janie said it was so obvious

that song was about her grandmother.

Did she really know? Was it really obvious?

Or did she read it on the Internet /

did the Internet even exist.

That feminism has been getting kind of retro lately,

maybe it's not the first time.

I take a selfie in the bathroom mirror

with a pink headband holding my bangs back.

I'm growing out my bangs / it's retro

It's a nod to myself in high school.

A shout out to myself & that things are changing.

A powder blue t-shirt with velvet dragon decal on it.

A thing I wore to Lilith Fair

I thought, I really need a room of my own

If that's what it takes these days

To find yourself, your voice.

To actually be in the woods.

If we got married

In the woods, like hippies but not.

Like feminists / in the sad gay 90s.

Things that Make Me Cry:

I thought I wanted to be

the other girls but maybe I don't.

I imagine my karaoke rendition of "Galileo," it floors you.

I imagine my rendition of "Possession" by Sarah McLachlan

and I'm shaking my ass & it's so smart

& I'll never sleep.

That scene in the show

where they're triumphantly singing along to the Indigo Girls

in the car on the way to the women's music festival.

& you might feel a shaft of light make its way across your face.

I want my room to be so full of light.

So 90s it makes the song skip.

DIARY

I have a two-part ring that he gave to me

when I was seventeen.

Flip it around. The bottom part is me now.

Lacy changed what she actually dressed like

in the 90s to be more girly for the 90s party.

My locker combo did this to me.

Ask not why you weren't in a band in high school

but why you don't start a band right now.

If I surround myself with all the most positive people it

will be as though I started a band in high school metaphorically.

Sister / Resister / Cape Cod / Colonial

I'm obsessed with the past and

you're obsessed with the present.

It's so boring. I saw a ghost.

I was always looking for things that were

the perfect blend of us together.

Us us us us us us. You you you you me me me me.

Jean-Luc Godard book & Jackie O sunglasses.

Corner next to the post office.

John & Yoko. Ross & Rachel.

Texting you I'm sorry.

Burning my diary.

Making you a copy

on CD.

When I'm staring at a baby

and their mom is looking back at me.

And there are giant hamburger emojis

where my eyes should be.

The TA I had in college

who asked what poetry I liked to read.

I said Frank O'Hara, unconfidently.

And for some reason he *laughed* at me.

The part of *Fast Times at Ridgemont High* when Linda says,

"Stacey, he's not a guy. He's a little prick!"

We were laughing so hard in church

mom told us we were going to hell, then we did.

When they're on a movie call in *Back to the Future 2*.

When my iPhone sends out an old email from

October that says "running late be there in ten!"

& it's like I never got there

& also like I'm still on my way.

You Turn Me On I'm a Yellow Sony Walkman

I like being a little bit mean to Stephen.

Wearing things that look architecture-y.

Eating apple pie with my ice cream.

I guess I couldn't help it.

I imagined my wedding brunch

on the tabletop catalog spread

I was writing called "A Perfect Match."

A girl at the work party asks me

where I live in New York City

I don't live there, I don't live anywhere.

Clip art of a nine-year-old

girl climbing a tree

leaning on her elbow

skinning her knee

VP of Creative sending an email

with the subject line "The Future"

You calling my tampon a little mouse

as you pulled it out

DIARY

I'm wearing my FUPA like this

cause it's part of my outfit

& also I'm wearing six necklaces.

I'm floating down the stairs.

Emily Dickinson poem

flanked by ads for Spanx

and Neutrogena, tours of

haunted Salem homes.

Guess I'm doing okay.

Had an opportunity but missed it.

Ran for the train but missed it.

Layering on the nonexistent lipstick

like I'm going to my first bat mitzvah

Unicorn nail decal

Body dysmorphia like please.

My tits sag but these

aren't my tits.

You in black and white.

Your boyfriend's four fingers.

Walking backwards

in a field of green grass, 1993.

I'm at a party I'm in seventh grade

and "I Swear" by All-4-One is playing.

And I keep saying that I hate it,

but really I love it.

And I keep saying that it's a metaphor

but it's not a metaphor.

It's a Rorschach / an inkblot on my extra-large

Maxi pad with wings /

the wings are a metaphor for freedom.

I wanted to be a size zero.

I wanted to not exist at all.

Selfie in the Event of Time Still Rapidly Passing.

You could come over.

It could be the 90s.

We could lie outside w/ Sun In in our hair.

Plastic Easter egg w/ a twenty in it.

Woke up stoked then killed it.

Running outside listening to Monster Ballads playlist

J texts me at the exact first second of "Every Rose Has its Thorn."

Poem After One Jack & Ginger While Home Alone Listening to Steve Miller Spotify Station

When you're away I send you bride emojis.

I text Seth wait is "Riders on the Storm"

the worst song ever written

when probably the whole world is sleeping.

Gonna wake my neighbors it's so embarrassing

"Landslide" comes on but I can't sing

cause my voice hurts too much.

I told Seth the Smashing Pumpkins cover

was the first version I ever heard.

(He said, oh woah.)

In "Stairway to Heaven" when he says,

there's a feeling I get when I look to the west.

Is he talking about California?

Cause I was.

Favorite thing about *Wayne's World*: No Stairway

or how my dad quotes the Alice Cooper part sometimes

or how I want to write in all my vacuum copy

"this vacuum certainly does suck."

Favorite thing about Becca:

That her favorite movie is *Wayne's World*

or that she's into Zack Morris Cell Phone as a poetry aesthetic.

Prompt: finish the poem before "Stairway" ends.

I'm making a dance in my kitchen to "Purple Haze."

More like an elaborate cheer or color guard routine.

Marching in place w/ flags.

Ew the album cover for *Hotel California* is

an actual hotel in California it's disgusting.

Were the 80s disgusting?

Was it disgusting when I was born?

Bride after bride like some chick

with sooooooooo many husbands.

My emojis don't even work,

I have to google "moon emoji" to say goodnight to Seth.

it's so Zack Morris Cell Phone to talk about it.

Favorite thing about Seth:

That *The Big Lebowski*'s on Netflix

or that I have a log of our AOL Instant Messenger

conversations somewhere on my computer.

iPhone doesn't autocorrect AOL and it's like, respect yr elders.

Favorite thing about Dave:

How he alienated the whole class

of UMass incoming freshman

when he emceed me and Heather's *Saved by*

the Bell trivia at the orientation talent show.

How I kept a condom in my wallet

like some fucking jock finger.

How we grew up into better versions.

The sluttiest underwear I own are the ones

my mom put in my Easter basket.

Woulda gone to bed early but I'm

still up up up up up up up up up up up up up shout out to Ani.

How did we become poets, what a stupid destiny.

How in the summer sometimes I'd lie in bed,

listen to the birds fly overhead.

Shout out to "Brain Damage/Eclipse."

New moon emoji.

DIARY

I hate this sweater but I'm too cold not

to wear it as a metaphor for my career.

My therapist says yes corporations take advantage

of human beings' ambitious nature.

My insurance says they will cover

zero dollars for our visits.

What a thrill. I cut my finger while washing the blender

at the exact second that I think of you.

We went to the protest, I bought those powder

blue shoes with the green alligator on them.

Handmaid's Tale jokes at the VMAs. Clean versions of songs.

Picking out baby names for babies that will never be born.

You bought the diamond necklace for mom at the mall,

you have great taste. You bought it at a store called Accessory Place.

Recurring nightmare that I missed the whole summer.

Walks I took on my lunch break with Heather.

Grunge deaths. Being in the dark. Nail art.

Chris Brown playing on Rihanna Spotify station.

I go into the bathroom, I say "great tits" to myself in the mirror.

How can you expect your nail polish to look glossy

when you don't even put on a top coat you stupid bitch.

I was in the infant/toddler room.

I was eating peanut butter & banana.

Fuming with rage at the galleria.

D was like, maybe it will be our Vietnam.

I'm so sad. No one cares.

Tampons with applicators.

Tampons without applicators.

A maxi pad called Always.

Blasting the car radio.

The guy at the McDonald's drive-thru who told you

your hair was the exact same color as your eyes.

M texts me a picture of a baby goose

we rescued from a river.

I buy the makeup the guy in the store tells

me he wears every day. It's pink & shiny.

Run into Sharon at Park and 22nd

Run into Sharon in the 8th grade hallway

Wake up in the morning, I have that feeling

like if aliens landed on the planet they

would think that capitalism was a horror movie.

Gently used Louboutins

Fainted in the elevator while carrying

a dozen eggs, broke them all

I'm walking around H&M with a frown on my face

like a poster girl for the fact that money can't buy happiness.

A utopia where all the coders are pretty girls with vocal fry

My therapist said "whoomp there it is" about loneliness.

Standing on the street corner, waiting for my life to change

Look up at the sky / tendrils of clouds

JK look back down

NOTES

"Remember Me"
"Remember Me" takes its name from the 90s young adult horror book by Christopher Pike.
"But I wasn't a bad girl…" is a line from Christopher Pike's book.
"Went from a little to a lot this year" is a lyric from Jennifer Lopez's "Jenny from the Block."

Spring Is Here Again
"Spring is here again" is a lyric from the Nirvana song "In Bloom."
"Turning passers-by to stone w/ my bald eye" is a reference to the Louise Bogan poem "Medusa."
"Holy Sonnet" takes its name from John Donne's Holy Sonnets.
"Sad tomato" is a line from the R.E.M. song "Crush with Eyeliner."
"They really want you but I do too." is a lyric from the Hole song "Doll Parts."
"Where have all the good men gone / & where are all the gods." is a lyric from "I Need a Hero" by Bonnie Tyler.
"Love it in yr room at night" is a lyric from the Bangles song "In Your Room."
"In the dark I like to read his mind" is a lyric from "Voices Carry" by 'Til Tuesday.
The Zack Morris Cell Phone Aesthetic is a poetic philosophy that Becca Klaver and I invented and that nobody's ever heard of.
"Caught a lite sneeze," "pieces of me you've never seen," and "tear in my hand" are lyrics from the Tori Amos songs "Caught a Light Sneeze" and "Tear in Your Hand."
"Friends Forever" is a song from the TV show *Saved by the Bell*.
"& that's what sad is" is a reference to the Alice Notley poem "A True Account of Talking to Judy Holiday, October 13."

Big Brown Bag

"Cause I'm cool like that" is a lyric from "Rebirth of Slick" by Digable Planets.

"Somebody's 'Heine'" is a lyric from "Say It Ain't So" by Weezer.

"Don't tell them to grow up, and out of it" is a lyric from "Changes" by David Bowie.

Diary

"I wanna fly down over Mulholland" is a lyric from the Tom Petty song "Free Fallin'."

"Problem w/o a name" is a reference to "the problem that has no name" from Betty Friedan's *The Feminine Mystique*.

"That I would be good" and "That I would be good even if I got the thumbs down." are from the Alanis Morissette song "That I Would Be Good."

"There's no one left to finger" is a lyric from the Sarah McLachlan song "Adia."

"& you might feel a shaft of light make its way across your face." is a lyric from the 10,000 Maniacs song "These Are Days."

"I have a two part ring..." references the Louise Bogan poem "The Crossed Apple."

"My locker combo did this to me" references Jack Spicer's last words, "My vocabulary did this to me."

"You Turn Me On I'm a Yellow Sony Walkman" is a reference to Joni Mitchell's "You Turn Me On I'm a Radio"

"Up up up up up" is the name of an Ani DiFranco album.

"Brain Damage/Eclipse" is a Pink Floyd song (technically two songs).

"What a thrill. I cut my finger while washing the blender" references the Sylvia Plath poem "Cut."

"Standing on the street corner, waiting for my life to change" is a lyric from "Damn, I Wish I Was Your Lover" by Sophie B. Hawkins.

ACKNOWLEDGEMENTS

Many thanks to the editors of the following publications, where earlier versions of these poems were published: *The Nation, Wonder, Blush Lit, Peach Mag, Boog City, So and So, EOAGH, Prelude, As It Ought to Be, Moonshot, Ghost Town, Yes Femmes, Bedfellows, No, Dear,* and *By the Slice* (Spooky Girlfriend, 2014). The poems in Big Brown Bag also appeared in the chapbook *Big Brown Bag*, which was selected by Natalie Diaz as the winner of the Fall for the Book prize and published by Gazing Grain Press in 2015. Thanks to Natalie Diaz and to the editors, Alyse Knorr and Kate Partridge, and the rest of the Gazing Grain team. Thank you to Small Press Traffic and This Will Take Time's residency program.

Thank you to all of my writer friends and literary community who have inspired, read, given feedback on, and supported these poems and my writing in so many ways: Becca Klaver, Seth Landman, Caolan Madden, Jenni(f)fer Tamayo, MC Hyland, Truong Tran, Megan Milks, Eleanor C. Whitney, Naomi Extra, Chrissy Hernandez, Monica McClure, Forsyth Harmon, Emily Brandt, Marina Weiss, Amy Berkowitz, Beth Pickens, Michelle Tea, Julián Delgado Lopera, Lily Ladewig, Hanna Andrews, Morgan Parker, Geraldine Kim, Kate Durbin, and many others.

Thank you to Erin M. Riley for this book's beautiful cover art.

Thank you to Heather Woods, T Thilleman, and the rest of the Spuyten Duyvil team for giving this work a home.

Thank you to my family. Thank you to my friends. Thank you to Matt L Roar.

MARISA CRAWFORD is the author of the poetry collections *Reversible* and *The Haunted House*. She is co-editor, with Megan Milks, of *We Are The Baby-Sitters Club: Essays & Artwork from Grown-Up Readers,* and editor of *The Weird Sister Collection* (Feminist Press, forthcoming 2024). Marisa's writing has appeared in *The Nation, Harper's Bazaar, Hyperallergic, BUST*, and elsewhere. She lives in New York.

Printed in Great Britain
by Amazon

31651891R00052